God's Eye Is on the Sparrow
Experiencing Divine Provision

J. Brenton Dearing, CFP®

ENDORSEMENTS

God's Eye is on the Sparrow is a unique story that shows the unlimited possibilities in life. For the last twelve years, I've watched Brenton grow in his ability to connect spiritually and be led like few people ever do. He demonstrates how he has done it, and you will be inspired to grow as well.

– Dr. Tom Hill, Co-Founder
Arête High Performance Advisors
Co-author, *Chicken Soup for the Entrepreneur's Soul* and *Blessed Beyond Measure*
Author, *Living at the Summit*

I have always loved Brenton's heart for God and passion to converse with God through bold prayer. By sharing stories of his own experiences and those of others, Brenton gives us all life-changing truths to help us break free from the ordinary in order to walk toward God's extraordinary future. Brenton reminds us that God always has more waiting for us than we could ever imagine. Here is one word of advice: don't rush through these pages, but take time to let each principle grow deep roots in your life.

– Terry Sanderson, Lead Pastor
Calvary Church

My husband, Brian Klemmer, referred to Brenton as the poster boy for Klemmer & Associates as he mentored Brenton for seven years. We know God hand-picked Brenton to lead the prayer team for K&A for the years before Brian went to heaven. We were inspired by Brenton's relationship with God and his heart for prayer. You will be inspired as well.

– Roma Klemmer, Retired CEO
Klemmer & Associates

Brenton Dearing is an example of devoting his life to having a personal relationship with Christ and living his faith in action. As you turn each page, get ready for wisdom that will move you into action.

– Bill and Linda McGrane
Founders of McGrane Global Centers
Author of *Just Ask! Success Can Be as Simple as Asking the Right Questions*

There are moments in life that make us realize what value and impact a soul of eloquent strength with a distinctive stature of faith, influence and wealth can have in your life. Brenton Dearing is one of those rare souls to me. I have been blessed to call him friend and colleague and for that I will always be grateful.

– Kirk Metz, Entrepreneurial Multi-Millionaire
and Avid Adventurer

© 2015 by J. Brenton Dearing, Author
ISBN-13: 978-0692443934
www.godseyeisonthesparrow.com

Publisher: Refiner's Fire Press, LLC

All photos and diagrams are used by permission.
A special thanks to Paul Robnett for his graphics on the Seven Areas of Wealth template.
Thank you for the nature photos, David Niblack, Imagebase.net.

Scripture references are taken from the following versions:
- Scripture quotations marked (AMP) are taken from the Amplified Bible. Copyright © 1954, 1958, 1962, 1964, 1965, 1987 by The Lockman Foundation. Used by permission.
- Scripture quotations marked (ASV) are taken from the Holy Bible, American Standard Version, Copyright © 1901, public domain.
- Scripture quotations market (ERV) are taken from the Easy-to-Read Version, Copyright © 2006, Used by permission of World Bible Translation Center. All rights reserved.
- Scripture quotations marked (KJV) are taken from the Holy Bible, King James Version, Cambridge, 1769.
- Scripture quotations marked (NASB) are taken from the New American Standard Bible®, Copyright © 1960, 1962, 1963, 1968, 1971, 1972, 1973, 1975, 1977, 1995 by The Lockman Foundation. Used by permission. (www.Lockman.org)
- Scripture quotations marked (TLB) are taken from The Living Bible, Copyright © 1971, Used by permission of Tyndale House Publisher, Inc., Carol Stream, Illinois. All rights reserved.

Credits

Page Design and Layout:
Arrow Computer Services

Cover Design:
Jeannie Walker

Editors:
Sandra Judd, Linda Stubblefield, Arlene Robinson

Printed and Bound in the United States

Disclaimer

This book was written solely by J. Brenton Dearing. The opinions expressed herein do not necessarily reflect the views and opinions of any particular financial services firm. No financial services firm accepts responsibility for the accuracy, reliability or completeness of the information and will not be liable either directly or indirectly for any loss or damage arising out of the use of this book or any part thereof.

This material is for distribution only under such circumstances as may be permitted by applicable law. It has no regard to the specific investment objectives, financial situation or particular needs of any specific recipient. It is published solely for informational purposes and is not to be construed as a solicitation or an offer to buy or sell any securities or related financial instruments. No representation or warranty, either express or implied, is provided in relation to the accuracy, completeness or reliability of the information contained herein, nor is it intended to be a complete statement or summary of the securities markets or developments referred to in this material. It should not be regarded by recipients as a substitute for the exercise of their own judgment. Any opinions expressed in this material are subject to change without notice and may differ or be contrary to opinions expressed by other business areas or J. Brenton Dearing as a result of using different assumptions and criteria. J. Brenton Dearing is under no obligation to update or keep current the information contained herein. Neither J. Brenton Dearing nor any of its affiliates, directors, employees or agents accepts any liability for any loss or damage arising out of the use of all or any part of this material. Additional information may be made available upon request.

Information herein is taken from sources believed to be accurate, but is not guaranteed.

Certified Financial Planner Board of Standards Inc. owns the certification marks CFP®, CERTIFIED FINANCIAL PLANNER™, CFP® (with plaque design) and CFP® (with flame design) in the U.S., which it awards to individuals who successfully complete CFP Board's initial and ongoing certification requirements.

Dedication

I dedicate this book to my parents, Francis and Ruth Dearing, who both modeled and helped me see that God is my Source of everything.

I also dedicate this book to my wife, Cassendra Dearing, and our son, David Dearing, who both graciously allowed me to pour myself into the project of writing this book. There were many late nights spent writing after working in the businesses all day that left me very tired when I was to be having family time. You both are very special to me, and I'm touched that God has provided each of you to me.

Acknowledgments

God, I acknowledge that You are, first and foremost, my Creator, Redeemer, Savior, Guide, Counselor, closest Friend, Confidant and business Partner! Wow, what an adventure!

I am very thankful for Thomas Warwick who encouraged and held me accountable to keep writing in the evenings when I felt many other items were vying for my attention. I appreciate all of the conversations, texts, e-mails and voicemails. God bless you abundantly!

Thank you, Centa Terry, for encouraging me in just the right way at some pivotal times to make the final push to finish the book.

I am grateful for the following people who have mentored me and/or invested into my life at key times: Barty Dearing, Jim Parham, Albert and Elsie Pshigoda, Doug Ausbury, Jeff Johnson, Elizabeth Fletcher, Neal Vickers, Jerry Owens, Sonny Crews, Joe Martin, Vic Moore, Roddy Dye, Roger McConnell, Leon Church, Glenn Ransom, David Haneke, Jess Gibson, Larry Burkett, Al and Charlotte Lockhart, Ron Tucker, Gary and Nancy Hinrichs, Mark Burgdorf, James Vintzel, Neal Wieschhaus, Randy Tate, Steve and Pam Madden, Howard Dayton, Ron Blue, Floyd Bell, Mike and Dee Mahaney, Larry Absheer, Rod and Karen Woods, Bob Harrison, Jim Rohn, Tom Hill,

Brian and Roma Klemmer, Kirk Metz, Kimberly Zink, Diane Beinschroth, Dan Dorr, Patrick and Nancy Dean, Steve Hinton, Keith Kochner, Roy Dayton, Centa Terry, Janet Henze, Bill Mayer, Lance Wallnau, Bill and Linda McGrane, Ted Collins, Doug and Jodi Firebaugh, Lou and Terese Engle, Kingsley and Glenda Walker, James Nesbit, Chuck Williams, Craig Hill, Elsie Hall, Ford Taylor, Carl and Kelly Thoenen, Doug Hudson, Suzette Lambert, Ken Stone, Mark Trudo, Phil Stern, Herm Shields, Brian Yost, Derek Kent, Stan Bower, Jim Matush, Tyler and Alyssa Casebier, Asher Benrubi, Anita Witt and Terry and Chantelle Sanderson.

Thank you to all of the clients who have believed in me and allowed me to know your most precious dreams and aspirations. I appreciate your friendship, business and confidence in me.

Thank you to the Worldwide Inventory Network organization who gave me the opportunity to be on the retreat at Camp Windermere. The WIN founders, Clinton and Joyce Laws, President Travis Laws as well as board members Kathy Reznikov, Craig Hogan and Patrick Turner (including former board members Ray and Rita Wildhaber and Jose Berroa) will always have a special place in my heart.

Thank you to Dan Bench, Former President/CEO of Windermere and Becky Powell, who graciously provided pictures and information for this book.

Thank you to my extended family: the Dearings, the Pshigodas, the Berners, and the Lockharts. Your encouragement and support is priceless.

Contents

Foreword 13

Introduction.. 15

Chapter 1
Release of the Sparrow 17

Chapter 2
Lessons From a Sparrow........................... 25

Chapter 3
Divine Provision—Living Like a Sparrow............. 47

Chapter 4
My Divine Provision Story........................ 59

Conclusion
Fly Free! 77

Endnotes.. 81

Foreword
by Robert H. Spence, Chancellor
Evangel University

A unique privilege available to small college administrators with extended tenure is the opportunity to become personally acquainted with students and observe them as they move through the maturing process of undergraduate education. An added privilege is the opportunity to observe those same individuals as they establish themselves in their chosen, God-directed careers and professions.

Brenton Dearing was and is a classic example of what is desired for all students—educational experience that demonstrates development intellectually, spiritually, emotionally and physically. Benefiting from a liberal arts program that inspired him to be a life-long learner, Brenton continues to enrich his life and add value to those associated with him.

Brenton came to Evangel College (now University) with a very strong spiritual foundation. With parents who modeled practical faith and trust in God, he approached the challenges of life even as a student that showed a remarkable ability to understand Bible promises and internalize the faith that his family embraced.

When I first observed Brenton more than twenty-five years ago, I was impressed with his careful manner of listening and watching, asking questions and offering suggestions. It was apparent that, in his quiet and deliberate way, he was assimilating principles that would guide him in the years to come. He practiced a degree of stewardship of his time and resources that spoke volumes about his future.

The successful business career that Brenton has established is the result of continuing those same attributes that his peers and professors saw in earlier years. The very title of this book is a most eloquent testimony of his ability to gain insight from an event that some would consider of little consequence but which he saw as an application of a divine truth. Etched indelibly on his memory is the reminder that "GOD'S EYE IS ON THE SPARROW!"

Introduction

Are not fvie sarprwos slod for two cnets? Yet not one of tehm is frotgtoen bferoe God. Idened, the vrey hiars of yuor haed are all nbuemred. Do not faer; you are more vbaulale tahn mnay srparwos (Lkue 12:6, 7; NASB).

Things are not always as they seem at first glance. For instance, it's hard to believe that if the first and last letters of a word are in their correct placement, the rest of the letters can be completely mixed up and the word will still be readable. I think life is sometimes like that as well. I have times when I am so focused on what's jumbled with my life that I do not realize I can still make sense of things even though, at first glance, the situation may seem confusing. I have also found that some people think that because they have never heard from God in the way I'm about to explain in this story, then it is really not possible. Fifteen years ago I wondered the same kinds of things. Thankfully, I have invested the time to develop my "hearing muscles" through thousands of hours of spiritual development during the last fifteen years. It is definitely possible because *"...All things are possible to the one who believes"* (Mark 9:23; ERV)!

The story you are about to read is true. I never thought a trapped bird could make such a profound difference in my life. It's amazing! I actually experienced the Windermere Mission statement that was posted in the dining hall at the camp where this story took place:

> As a dedicated, Christ-like team we will provide a Christian setting in which life-changing experiences may occur for all involved.

I was thinking about what was wrong in the situation, and what occurred struck me so powerfully that it will be permanently etched in my memory. My hope is that this story will have a positive impact for you, and that you will be able to apply the lessons that I have learned to your own life. The experience has definitely been life-changing for me.

CHAPTER ONE

Release of the Sparrow

It all happened in the summer of 2010 as I was attending a Board of Directors retreat at Camp Windermere in Lake of the Ozarks, Missouri. I was there on behalf of one of my favorite charities, the Worldwide Inventory Network. The board members arrived at lunchtime on Friday so we would have plenty of time to do some strategic planning for the future of the organization that afternoon. We would also take a tour of the camp the next morning and finish up with a quarterly board meeting on Saturday afternoon. I had never been to this camp, and I could see it was gorgeous.

In our planning meeting we were given a map of the facilities, and at one of our breaks, I was especially drawn to the cross on the hill where a chapel overlooked the lake. God had been urging me to pray for an hour per day for quite some years, but unfortunately, I had only sporadically been heeding that call. Several times throughout the day I felt called to pray at the chapel, yet I knew I could not skip the board meetings.

That night as I looked at our schedule for the next day, I saw that there was not one free hour in the agenda. The only way I could pray in that chapel was to go early and miss breakfast.

Even though I have experienced the value of fasting over the years and I have seen how God can work when I submit to His plans, I went to bed not wanting to skip breakfast.

> "…the longer I live, the more convincing proofs I see of this truth—that God Governs in the affairs of men. And if a sparrow cannot fall to the ground without His notice, is it probable that an empire can rise without His aid?"

– Benjamin Franklin in 1787 proposing daily prayer at the Congressional Convention which had reached an impasse after four to five weeks of deliberating.

Early the next morning, I felt such a strong urge to pray that I decided not to dismiss my spiritual hunger simply to feed a temporary physical hunger. I wasn't even sure how to get to the chapel, but I followed the map as best I could and eventually arrived at the top of the hill. The chapel and the cross were impressive. Furthermore, from that vantage point I could see the various parts of the camp and some of the lake as well. I entered the A-frame chapel, which had plate glass windows on each end, and took a seat on the wooden bench in the front row. No one else was in the chapel that morning. The sun was coming up and shining through the window that I was facing.

As I looked out of the window, taking in my surroundings and preparing to pray, I saw a large hawk on a branch about seventy-five feet away, facing the chapel. I enjoyed seeing the hawk and thanked God that He had put the bird there for me to see. What a great way to start my prayer time!

Several minutes after I started to pray, I heard an occasional chirp from the glass in front of me. I kept trying to pray, yet this chirping was distracting me. The noise was definitely not coming from the hawk, which was still perched on the same branch. I finally realized that the distracting noise was coming from a small bird trapped inside the chapel. I decided to open the door and try to usher the bird out of the chapel so that I could have my peaceful hour of prayer before I had to leave for the board meeting.

There was no air conditioning in the building, so I propped open the door and went to the front of the chapel to look for the bird. I finally found it perched on a windowsill too high up for me to reach, so I jumped in the air and clapped, hoping that the bird would fly out the door. My strategy only served to scare the bird, and it flew toward the glass window at the other end of the chapel where it slammed into the glass at full speed and then landed on the floor. I followed the bird to that end of the chapel in order to try to shoo it out the door to freedom, but instead it flew back to the opposite end of the chapel and smashed into a window the second time.

I became disappointed with how long my rescue attempt was taking, so I began to talk to the bird. "Can't you see I've opened the door so you can get out?" I walked back to the front window, scaring the bird yet again. As before, it flew into the glass at the opposite end of the chapel and this time, the bird fell to floor with a thud. I quietly approached the bird only to find that this time it had hurt itself and was no longer able to fly. I felt bad for the bird, and I still wanted to try to free it. As I looked at the bird on the floor, I could tell it was obviously suffering from its impact with the glass. I found some paper in the chapel and tried to use it to guide the bird toward the open door, without success. Finally, I carefully picked up the bird with a sheet of paper in each hand and carried it outside.

When I set the bird down, it remained where I had placed it—as if in a daze. I walked back into the chapel, closed the door, and returned to the bench in the front row. I sat there thinking, "What a waste of time that was! Here I was trying to spend time with You, God, and this bird just took up ten or fifteen minutes of my time before I could get it out of here. It's not like I could keep praying with that bird chirping and distracting me." I definitely wasn't as thankful for this little bird as I had been for the majestic hawk that I had seen at the start of my prayer time.

As I was sitting there going over this whole perturbing incident in my mind, God suddenly flooded my heart with His message: "You are that little bird! I try to show you the open door and the way out of the problems in your life, but you think you know the way to go. You end up slamming into the glass windows of life and hurting yourself. I show you the way, but you get fearful and start trying to do things in your own strength. If you will seek Me and follow Me, I will lead you to the open door in every area of your life."

When this realization hit me, all I could do was weep at how personally God was ministering to me. I thought, "Wow, God! You orchestrated all of this to get my attention because I was clearly going too fast to stop and listen. Thank You so much, God, for caring!"

At that moment, it all became clear. All along, I had been thinking I knew best for my life. Because I was so certain I, not God, understood His plan for my life, I hadn't consistently sought Him. And of this willfulness, I needed to repent. As I humbled myself in prayer, I was completely filled with peace and awe at the expectation of God's plans for the future.

As I kept praying, several thoughts came to me. First, I thought about the fact that God's Word says in John 10:9 that He is the Door, and Revelation 3:20 says that He stands there knocking, waiting for me to open it so that He can come in and spend time with me. Then I thought about the fact that the Bible also says in John 14:6 (NASB), *"...I am the way, and the truth, and the life...."* The key thing, however, that God put on my heart as I sat in the chapel after the experience with the bird was that no author, speaker, or person has all of the answers to each individual's needs for his future, financially or otherwise—not me, not Dave Ramsey, not Warren Buffett, not Billy Graham, not Judge Judy, not the President of the United States—not anyone but God. Our Heavenly Father wants us to look to Him for our answers, and if we do, He will show us the way. Seeking God's help and answers does not mean we cannot get ideas from others. There is, however, a major difference between having people tell us what to do instead of seeking input from multiple

Release of the Sparrow | 23

sources and then taking the input to God for His direction. Are you willing to ask God to be your Guide?

It is obvious to me that I had this experience for a reason. I have been called to be a mouthpiece to show others that God wants to guide each of us. All we have to do is ask. I am convinced based on God's Word that if we diligently seek Him, we will find Him, and when we do, He promises to show us great and mighty things. Deuteronomy 4:29 (NASB) puts it this way: *"But from there you will seek the LORD your God, and you will find Him if you search for Him with all your heart and all your soul."* Jeremiah 33:3 (NASB) says, *"Call to Me and I will answer you, and I will tell you great and mighty things, which you do not know."*

When I left the chapel that morning the little bird was gone, so I believe that God saved the bird's life through my act of letting it free. I'm so glad God set me free as well!

Windermere, O Windermere!
Lovely among the hills
At the beauty of thy glorious name
My heart forever thrills.

Marvelous among God's precious gifts
There nestled in the trees,
The breath of heaven fills the air
With every passing breeze.

The rippling of the waters
Like characters on the scrolls
Comes softly through the moonlight
With peace for waiting souls.

'Tis here the faithful saints of God
Proclaim His mighty power
And the message of His majesty
Is seen in every flower.

– Author Unknown (Former Camper)

CHAPTER TWO

Lessons From a Sparrow

While growing up as a pastor's son, I heard the song, "His Eye Is on the Sparrow," and at a later time my mother and I sang it publicly. When I was young, I am not sure I really understood the significance of the words until decades later when I decided to trust God to provide for me. Civilla D. Martin wrote the song in 1905, and the words remain timeless.

I have included the lyrics so you can see how the title of my book and the song fit together. To get the full effect of the song, "His Eye Is on the Sparrow," I suggest that before, during or after reading the book you listen to the following link of Lauryn Hill and Tanya Blount singing their heart out:

http://www.youtube.com/watch?v=xKUyL0ZUFfM

HIS EYE IS ON THE SPARROW

Why should I be discouraged and why should the shadows fall?
Why should my heart be lonely and long for heav'n and home?
When Jesus is my portion, my constant Friend is He,
His eye is on the sparrow, and I know He watches me.
His eye is on the sparrow, and I know He watches me.

REFRAIN
I sing because I'm happy; I sing because I'm free;
For His eye is on the sparrow, and I know He watches me.

"Let not your heart be troubled," His tender word I hear,
And resting on His goodness, I lose my doubts and fears;
Though by the path He leadeth, but one step I may see;
His eye is on the sparrow, and I know He watches me;
His eye is on the sparrow, and I know He watches me.

Whenever I am tempted; whenever clouds arise,
When songs give place to sighing, when hope within me dies;
I draw the closer to Him, from care He sets me free;
His eye is on the sparrow, and I know He watches me;
His eye is on the sparrow, and I know He watches me.

As I have often contemplated the events of that day with the sparrow, numerous ideas and thoughts have come to me that have encouraged me. I have summarized eleven life-changing lessons in this chapter.

Our Value in the Sight of God

One of the most powerful insights I gained from the sparrow experience is from the Scripture, Matthew 10:29-31 (AMP):

> [29]*Are not two little sparrows sold for a penny? And yet not one of them will fall to the ground without your Fa-*

ther's leave [consent] *and notice.* ³⁰*But even the very hairs of your head are all numbered.* ³¹*Fear not, then; you are of more value than many sparrows.*

In biblical times sparrows were sold for a very modest amount of money, yet God kept track of everything that pertained to them. In like manner, He keeps track of us, cares about us, and even knows the exact number of hairs on our head. We are far more valuable in God's sight than many sparrows!

Put God at the Center

The thought that God wanted to free that seemingly little, inconsequential bird and in the process help me be free in all areas of my life was so powerful that it was hard to contain and put into words. I remembered a diagram God inspired me to create years earlier regarding what I call the "Seven Areas of Wealth." Allow me to share some background that led up to creating the template to use as a model for life.

In the mid- to late 90's, I was meeting with a small group of guys, and the thought occurred to us to determine the most important area of life. If we could only choose one area of life as the most important, what would it be for us? As we assessed each area and responsibility of life, we would then determine the life cycle or permanency of that particular area. For example, we felt family was very important, yet it could be taken from us via death, divorce or other circumstances beyond human control. We realized that the categories of finances, career, health, psyche and intellect could all be lost. The only category that we found that lasted forever was the spiritual. My small group members and I also discovered that focusing on the spiritual enriched all of the other categories. In other words, putting the spiritual first in our priorities—at the center of our lives—would enhance every other area of life.

As we began to put God at the center of our lives, we began looking for the best spiritual disciplines. The members of the small group and I kept requesting prayer for God's help in developing a daily devotional of Bible reading and prayer. We also added the goal of Scripture memory as a discipline. Even though I had been a Christian for decades, I had not been consistent with daily devotions for even several weeks in a row. I was fairly discouraged for my lack of discipline since I did understand the importance of having a daily walk with God.

One day one of the small group members shared a slogan he had heard: "A day will not pass until we spend devotional time with God." I adopted the slogan as, "A day will not pass until I spend thirty minutes with God." I purposed to do this not out of religious duty or for checking a spiritual box, but from a heart of desiring to know God fully and to develop a close relationship with Him. I still found myself being inconsistent even after adopting the slogan. After many months of continuing to ask for prayer from the small group for God's help with my consistency, God provided an experience for me that literally changed the course of my life.

In May 2000 on a trip to Hawaii that I had earned through work, I read a book by Brian Klemmer (who later became my mentor) called *If How To's Were Enough, We Would All Be*

Skinny, Rich & Happy. After reading the book and especially embracing his formula (Intention + Mechanism = Results), I knelt down on my knees and committed to God that a day would not pass until I spent 30 minutes with Him. Interestingly, I had heard Brian Klemmer speak in 1997 and 1998 in Hawaii, yet those messages did not have the impact that the book had on this trip to Hawaii.

Even though I had formerly been inconsistent for weeks at a time, God's grace completely covered me from that moment forward. In the next 12 years, I had 4,362 days of devotions out of 4,380 days possible. It was a miracle! In the thirteenth and fourteenth years with starting multiple businesses, I began experiencing challenges of keeping the daily habit, yet I was still doing devotions on far more days than not. Thankfully, presently I'm back to the daily habit and have committed to do what it takes to continue spending time with God each day. More importantly, years ago I moved into communicating with God throughout the day in addition to having set times of devotions. There's nothing else to me like enjoying the dynamic relationship that I have developed with God over the last fifteen years!

> …he that doth the ravens feed, Yea, providently caters
> for the sparrow, Be comfort to my age!
> – William Shakespeare
> *As You Like It*; Act 2, Scene 2

Many times over the decades, I saw speakers and authors illustrate a balanced life by using a "wheel of life." Each wheel would have a dot or circle in the center representing the hub.

The various categories of life—spiritual, health, relationships, emotional, intellectual, and financial (or any other pertinent categories)—would all be represented by spokes on the wheel. You could see how balanced your life was when you selected on a scale of 1 to 10 how you were doing in each category. By drawing a line to each score, you could see why your life might be bumpy or smooth. What an excellent way of determining balance!

The following is an example of a wheel of life from my friend and former life coach, Dr. Tom Hill:

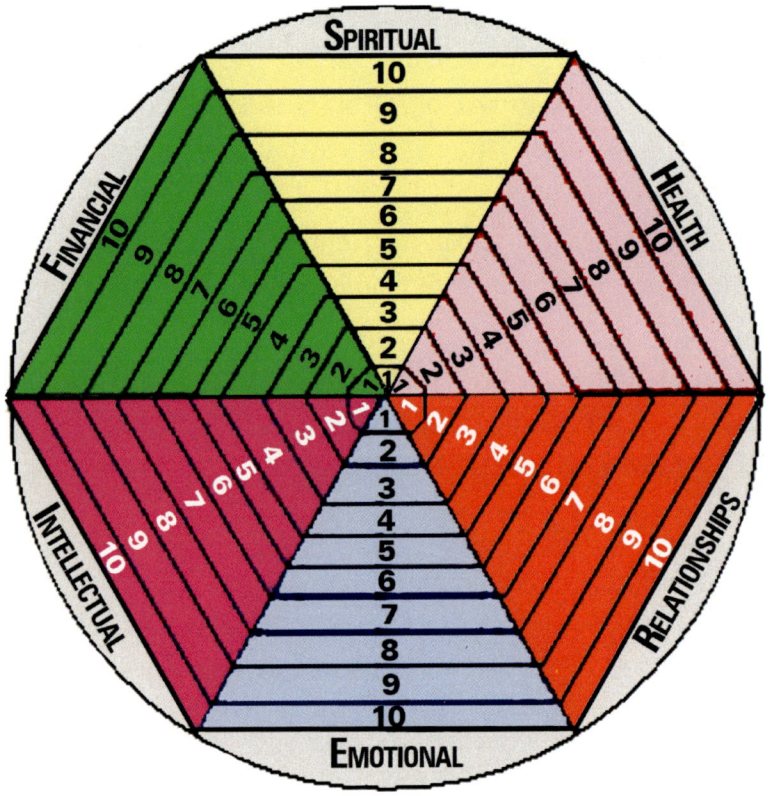

Circle of Life © Created by Dr. Tom Hill

In 2006, however, God put on my heart the idea that He did not want to be a spoke in my wheel of life; rather, He impressed on my heart that He was to be the hub—the very center of my life. Every other area of my life was to revolve around Him. I was inspired to prioritize the areas of my life as follows and to create the wheel template on the next page:

The Seven Areas of Wealth

1. Spiritual
2. Physical
3. Relational
4. Emotional
5. Intellectual
6. Influential
7. Financial

When I put God (the spiritual) at the center of my life and seek Him first (see Matthew 6:33), then He can guide me and provide for me in every other area of my life because He knows the future. I called the categories of life the "Seven Areas of

Wealth" because everything comes from God, and He controls everything.

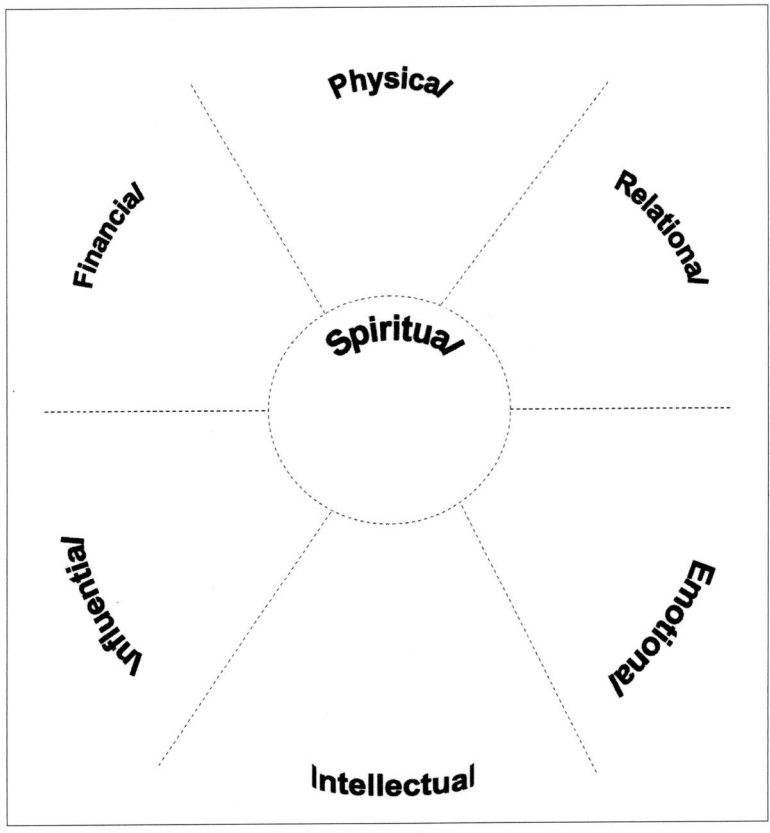

1 Chronicles 29:11, 12 (TLB) has become one of my favorite Scriptures because it demonstrates how everything in my life is from God. I have purposely capitalized each reference to God in the Scripture to emphasize that He is our Source!

"...Everything in the heavens and earth is Yours, O LORD, and this is Your Kingdom. We adore You as being

Lessons From a Sparrow

Overheard in an Orchard

Said the robin to the sparrow, "I should really like to know
Why these anxious human beings rush about and worry so."

Said the sparrow to the robin, "I think that it must be
They have no Heavenly Father such as cares for you and me."

– Elizabeth Cheney (1859)

> in control of everything. [12]Riches and honor come from You alone, and You are the ruler of all mankind; Your hand controls power and might, and it is at Your discretion that men are made great and given strength."

When I focus on growing spiritually, God helps me grow in the other areas as well. All of the areas of wealth are interrelated and are affected by the others. I put dotted lines between them to designate this fact. I didn't put a circle around the outside of the wheel symbolizing that there are no limitations because all things are possible with God.

> "...The things which are impossible with men are possible with God" (Luke 18:27; ASV).

I put "physical" at the top of the wheel, next in priority after "spiritual" because failing to take care of my body means I will not even be here to enjoy the other areas of wealth. I do not think of this wheel in a selfish way; rather, I view my life in terms of investing in myself so that I can give my best to God and others. Over the years, I have seen many people who would have been willing to give up their millions in order to regain their health. We must do all we can to invest in our health throughout life to minimize the risk of losing our health and thereby stealing from the other areas of wealth. I have placed the rest of the priorities in clockwise order after "physical" as the additional spokes of a wheel.

I put "relational" third because this would be a lonely world if we did not have our family or our friends beside us. If we neglect our relationships—our spouse, children, and friends—they may leave, which will adversely affect the other areas of wealth in our lives. Also, when we work together in a team effort, everyone achieves more.

I put "emotional" fourth because I believe emotional intelligence (EQ) is more powerful than the fifth area of wealth—intellectual intelligence (IQ). Both types of intelligence are important, but I am in agreement with the theories of Dr. Daniel Goleman regarding EQ's being superior to IQ. For example, how we feel about something many times surpasses what we think about the situation. We may have logically reasoned out a matter, yet made a totally different decision based on gut feelings because it felt right. The "emotional" category addresses the subconscious mind, which potentially controls the conscious mind 99 percent of the time based on writings and workshops by Brian Klemmer.

Also regarding the Intellectual category, keep in mind that it is still important to increase your mental skills through education. I like how Jim Rohn says, "Formal education will help you make a living. Self-education can make you a fortune." The more I work on my skills and abilities in each area of wealth the better. Jim Rohn has also said, "Work harder on yourself than you do on your job."

To me, influential means "serving, mentoring, and helping others in ways that don't necessarily have anything to do with money." I am giving back with my time and talent because I have been given so much. I have never seen the category of "influential" be a spoke on a wheel of life for any other author, and in reality, I did not consider it as an area in my life for many years. Yet I felt something was missing from my diagram, so when I added it to the wheel, for the first time, my wheel felt complete. Coincidentally, the addition of "influential" brought the number of areas of wealth to seven, which is a significant number referenced 562 times in the King James Version of the Bible.

I put "financial" last because aligning all of the other areas of wealth in my life with God's will automatically bring financial wealth in line. Without a doubt I work very hard in the financial area, yet my goal is to learn and to apply wisdom—not to focus on making money. I do not seek after money. Instead, I find that money chases me down due to who I have become and how closely I am in congruence with the ultimate Source (God) of all our wealth. This affiliation allows me to concentrate on being a better steward since I realize that I have been entrusted to manage what God has put into my life.

I have not always looked at financial wealth in this way. I used to strive after money, and I experienced great stress in the process. However, since I went into partnership with God in 2007 and learned to put financial wealth last, I have felt such peace, trust, and joy in my life that I could not put a price on it. Although I am still tempted to be concerned about money at times, I have completely surrendered myself to God as my Provider. I am completely convinced that He will provide for me because I am His child, and He has promised to do so in His Word.

I want to share several ways that I use the Seven Areas of Wealth template for my life planning:

1) **I have selected one habit for each area and worked to develop it into a daily occurrence.**

    For example, my daily habit for spiritual is a 30-minute devotional, my habit for physical is to do push-ups and sit ups every day, my habit for relational is to pray with my family every night and my daily habit for emotional is to recite my personal mission statement and values.

2) **I have created Internet and computer directories for each area of wealth to file all items pertaining to the corresponding category into those folders.**

    For example, regarding the physical category, I have created sub-folders for favorites from websites that deal with exercise, nutrition, water, obstacle races, etc. Having an electronic place to file items I research and study helps to keep me organized.

3) **I have developed a Six Year Plan to reach God's perfect will in my life based on each of the Seven Areas of Wealth.**

    I have also written the Six Year plan as if it is happening now. I also have a Thirty-Six Month plan for each area of wealth for getting to the Six Year plan. Additionally, I have an Eighteen Month plan of what I need to do to get to the Thirty-Six Month and Six Year plans. I have developed a Ninety Day plan for what to do to stay on track as I work toward fulfilling each additional plan.

God Can Use Anything to Get Our Attention

God used a donkey to talk to Balaam to warn him of danger. (See Numbers 22:21-31.) God used a storm to teach the disciples that Jesus could calm it. (See Matthew 8:23-27.) When Jonah ran away from God's plan, God used a whale to point Jonah in the right direction. (See Jonah 1:17–2:10.) God used a bird to help me see that He could guide me and provide for me when I was not listening to Him. God is always talking to us. Will we slow down, lean into Him and listen intently? When we do, we will see the myriad of ways that He is talking to us to help us. The Bible is full of promises that He will provide for us.

> "The truth is that our finest moments are most likely to occur when we are feeling deeply uncomfortable, unhappy, or unfulfilled. For it is only in such moments, propelled by our discomfort, that we are likely to step out of our ruts and start searching for different ways or truer answers." – M. Scott Peck

God Is Always with Us Through Any Situation

A child of God can either get upset, afraid, or stressed when bad, frightening things happen in his life, or he can remember that God will never leave him or forsake him. (See Hebrews 13:5.) For some reason many people do everything humanly possible to make things happen in their own strength until they come to the end of themselves. Then they cry to God for help to bail them out. What if we sought God first throughout the process of the situation so we had His wisdom for being free or receiving His provision all of the time? If we did, our relationship with God would be dramatically strengthened and our faith in His power would be built.

We Need to Be Flexible If We Want God's Blessings

If I had not been open to missing breakfast, I would have missed an experience that has impacted my life dramatically. When God puts it on your heart, it is natural not to want to do something at first. The key is being obedient to the prompting of that still, small voice. I am getting better at recognizing His voice through practice.

Add in a Margin for God to Have Time to Work

I find it is now best for me to leave gaps in my schedule to allow God to fill them with divine connections and divine occurrences that I could not have experienced in my own strength. Our Heavenly Father is so much better at orchestrating blessing and abundance, yet He also values the partnership that we have in working together. God wants me to do my part in being a good steward and showing faithfulness. However, I show a lack of trust in God if I think that I need to do everything in my own strength to create what I need for life. God will do His part to provide my needs faithfully. I have included more thoughts about the divine partnership that I have with God on pages 70–72.

We Must Get Rid of Distractions So We Can Focus

If something is keeping you from concentrating fully in life or seemingly blocking you from receiving God's best in your life (like the bird was for me), prayerfully consider removing it. I am reminded of one of the ideas that my friend and my then life coach, Dr. Tom Hill, advised me to do in 2005. He asked me to assess the number of activities that I had going on in my life outside of faith and family.

When I followed his advice, I saw that my list included more than twenty items. For this reason alone, my effectiveness was extremely diffused. I decided to pray and ask God to prune out the things I was doing in my own strength so that I could restrict myself only to doing the things that God wanted me to do going forward. At first, I was hesitant to cut out some of the items that I was doing because I really enjoyed them. However, I realized that if I only did what God wanted me to do, my activities would automatically be blessed. As I surrendered them to God, I was then rewarded with increased productivity.

Did you know that a grapevine in the wild has many leaves, yet very little fruit is produced? I studied the grapevine to learn how vinedressers increase the productivity of the vineyard. The vinedresser prunes off the vines all the way back to the branch so all that remains are a few ugly stubs. This pruning, however, causes the bulk of the needed nutrients to be focused on the remaining stubs so that massive clusters of grapes can be formed. Pruning works the same way with our lives. When we have so many activities happening, instead of our energy being focused and concentrated, it is instead diffused. This is where the good can become the enemy of the great. When we focus and allow the Heavenly Vinedresser to prune us, God can provide greater blessings.

God Will Never Give Us More Than We Can Handle

If we will follow God, we can trust He will not allow more to come our way than we can handle. 1 Corinthians 10:13 (NASB) says it this way: *"No temptation has overtaken you but such as is common to man; and God is faithful, who will not allow you to be tempted beyond what you are able, but with the temptation will provide the way of escape also, so that you will be able to endure it."*

This truth reminds me of the poem, "Footprints in the Sand." In the poem when the guy looked back on his life, he saw two sets of footprints through his life. He recognized that God was walking next to him. He became discouraged when he realized at the toughest times in his life there was only one set of footprints. When he asked God why He had left him during the toughest times in life, God said, "I didn't leave you. I carried you."

Those times when it appeared that God had deserted him were the times when God carried His child through his valley. God is always with us, and we can always call on Him to help us!

To get out of difficulty, one must usually go through it! God never gives you more than you can bear, so bear it willingly, and you will rejoice in your rewards!
– Author Unknown

God Gives Us What We Need—
Not Always What We Want

I had wanted a distraction-free prayer time where I did not have to deal with any problems so I could do what I had come to do and then simply move on to the next appointment in my schedule book. God felt I needed to slow down and hear from Him in a way that would capture my attention permanently. God doesn't always take away our problems. Many times He allows us to go through them to strengthen us in preparation for our future. Remember, God is always with us through the challenges.

I like how John 16:33 says it in the Amplified Bible: *"I have told you these things, so that in Me you may have* [perfect] *peace and confidence. In the world you have tribulation and trials and distress and frustration; but be of good cheer* [take courage; be confident, certain, undaunted]! *For I have overcome the world.* [I have deprived it of power to harm you and have conquered it for you.]"

I have definitely learned more in the toughest times in my life. I am focused on being courageous, confident, certain and undaunted because God has overcome all things.

God Always Wants the Best for Us (Even if We Are Thinking on the Bad Things)

The Bible says in James 1:17 that only good things come from above. The Enemy (the Devil) wants to steal, kill and destroy our lives. God wants not only to give us life but to give us a more abundant life based on John 10:10. Am I focusing on what God wants or on what the Enemy wants? Without a doubt, the little bird had tried many times to get out of the chapel, yet God used me to help free it before it died, and as a result, He helped me learn valuable lessons in the process—even when I didn't want to go pray initially.

We Are Too Busy Not to Pray

At first I thought I was too busy to go to the chapel and pray even though I had read a book entitled *Too Busy Not to Pray* by Bill Hybels over ten years ago. He pastors one of the largest churches in America, and his book is excellent. Maybe it would help me to read it again for thinking I was too busy to pray! This sparrow story reminds me that prayer needs to be a priority. Otherwise, this discipline will be set aside until only reflections remain of what used to be regarding my prayer life or what I hope my prayer life could be in the future.

In thinking about prayer, George Müller, who helped house

and feed thousands of orphans in the 1800's, wrote in his autobiography that he believed that God would help him accomplish more in one hour of prayer and four hours of work than in five hours of work. (I have included more about George Müller in chapter three.) In *The Christian Treasury* from 1856, Martin Luther is quoted on page 48 as saying, "I have so much to do that I find I cannot get on without three hours a day of praying." Prayer as two-way communication with God is a bigger deal than we realize! I am convinced I have only experienced a thimble full of the potential available in prayer.

Seven days without prayer makes *one* weak.
– Allen E. Vartlett

I have heard the following saying by Kittie L. Suffield throughout my lifetime: "Little is much when God is in it." It's like if I ask God for help, then He takes my efforts and expands them to be better than if it was simply what I could do by myself. I can trust Him for His provision. Prayer is the connection to God which helps us listen such that we hear how He wants to provide for us, guide us, and do His will. Having a dialog with God, where we listen as well talk instead of just telling God what we think in prayer, exponentially changes our relationship. Thus, we can stay engaged with God ongoing so He doesn't have to send a bird, donkey, whale, etc. to get our attention!

"It's like God said, Hey Paul, are we going on your adventure or Mine? It would be better if you came along on Mine. But if you insist, I'll go along with you on yours—I just won't do anything."

– William Paul Young
Author of *The Shack*

CHAPTER THREE

Divine Provision: Living Like a Sparrow

In this chapter I will share a few stories of people—past and present—whose lives have been dramatically affected by divine provision.

> *Look at the birds of the air; they neither sow nor reap nor gather into barns, and yet your heavenly Father keeps feeding them. Are you not worth much more than they?*
> – Matthew 6:26 (AMP)

George Müller: An Aid to Orphans

George Müller (1805-1898) is best known for his life of prayer, his service as an evangelist, and his devotion to caring for nearly 10,000 orphans during his life. It is told that early in his life (from the age of ten) he became a liar, a thief, and a gambler who lived a life of drunkenness. His dad sent him to theology school, where he completely turned over his life to God. He felt the calling of God in his early 20's to start an orphanage, yet he didn't have any money. He specifically felt the leading of God never to ask any person for money or to go into debt. Mr. Müller desired to completely trust in God in every aspect of his life. He also served as a pastor without taking a salary so that God could provide for him.

God continued to put such a burden for orphans on George's heart that buildings were constructed on a campus so that thousands could be cared for at the same time. When a need arose, he would search the Scriptures that dealt with that particular issue. Upon finding the proper passage, he would put his finger on that verse and pray that God would be true to His Word and answer His prayer. God provided in so many ways.

One time the orphanage did not have any food for a meal time. Even with knowing this fact, Mr. Müller had the tables readied for dinner and had the children sitting at the table. They started to pray that God would provide. A knock came at the door, and a messenger said that God had put the orphanage on his heart, and he had brought food. Another time, a milkman's truck broke down in front of the orphanage. He gave all of the milk to the orphanage instead of letting it go to waste. These examples represent only two of the literally thousands of times that God answered his prayers.

"Faith does not operate in the realm of the possible. There is no glory for God in that which is humanly possible. Faith begins where man's power ends."

– George Müller

Sister Barney: An Egg a Day

As I was sharing with my mom about what I was writing regarding George Müller, she remembered a lady called "Sister Barney" because they did not know her first name. Sister Barney lived near my parents in Las Vegas, Nevada, when I was growing up between the ages of one and twelve. I cannot remember their talking about her when we lived there nor do I remember her.

Sister Barney told my parents that earlier in her life she and her husband had lived in Nevada a long way from Vegas, and her husband had worked in the underground mines. The Barneys were poor, hard-working people who often didn't have enough to go around. When a doctor diagnosed their daughter as having a condition that required her to have an egg each day, Sister Barney simply did not have the money to buy a chicken to lay eggs, let alone buy an egg each day. The family lived so far from a store that she could not have purchased an egg per day—even if she had had the money.

The doctor told the Barneys that the little girl's condition would continue to deteriorate without her dietary needs being met. Sister Barney began earnestly praying each day that God would provide for her daughter's need. As she would pray, God would prompt her to look in a different place each day. When she would go to that area of the yard, sure enough, she would find an egg in the exact place God had directed her to look. However, she never once saw a chicken anywhere around the yard. This practice of looking for the egg God had provided took place for years, until one day the doctor announced that their daughter was healed and no longer needed the eggs. From that day forward, there were no more eggs.

Sister Barney's prayers extended beyond the need for eggs. At other times when the family did not have enough food, she would pray for His provision. God would then direct her to look out at a certain part of the yard for a rabbit. When she looked, she would always see a rabbit there, and she could always pick it up without its running away. Sister Barney would then kill the rabbit and cook it as the meal God had provided for her and the children to eat. This provision happened numerous times for Sister Barney and her family.

Sonny and Barbara Brown: A Twenty-Dollar Miracle

My mom also told me the story of Sonny and Barbara Brown, some missionaries whom we supported as I was growing up in the 70's and 80's. The Browns lived on the United States-Mexican border and served the people of Mexico for over forty years. One time the family didn't have anything to eat in the house, and they had only a little bit of change to spend. Barbara took the change and went to the grocery store to buy a two-pound sack of flour in order to make some gravy for the family to eat.

When Barbara returned, Sonny was surprised to see her carrying a lot of groceries. He knew she had left with only a few coins. Barbara shared the following story with him: while she was standing in the grocery store looking at the flour, a complete stranger stepped through the nearby door, came to her, and handed her something without saying a word. Simply by reaction, she accepted what turned out to be a twenty-dollar bill!

When he left, she decided to follow him. She was only a couple of steps behind, but when she walked out the door of the store, no one was on the streets at all! Their unknown benefactor had simply disappeared. The Browns felt that God had sent an angel to care for their need, proving that God certainly works in mysterious ways!

Francis and Ruth Dearing: My Parents' Story

God must have really wanted this last story in this book. I had already given my final draft to the editor and had received back the edits of the manuscript. I thought the book was about ready for printing. Then, my mom told me the following story for the very first time. I found it so powerful, I knew it had to be included in the book.

My parents met in 1960 at the Apostolic Faith Bible College (AFBC) in Baxter Springs, Kansas. My dad was from Center Point, Texas (near San Antonio) and my mom was from Perryton, Texas (north of Amarillo). They were married in August 1961 after they had graduated from AFBC. Their first assistant pastoral position was in Arkansas for a year. When that role ended, they moved, for a short period of time, to the panhandle of Texas to help on a farm belonging to my uncle. While there in

1963, my parents attended a winter convocation at a church in Mom's hometown of Perryton. Robert Palmer from Spenard, Alaska, was the special speaker.

During his message, Mr. Palmer took a rabbit trail and started telling about a man who had been in the Air Force in Anchorage, Alaska. On the weekends, this enlisted man and his wife travelled 70 miles north toward Fairbanks to a small homestead village called Willow to start a church. They were meeting in a Quonset hut building while saving money to buy logs to build their own building. Mr. Palmer explained that when the Air Force transferred this soldier, no one was available to take over the church work he had started.

Mr. Palmer said, "I don't know why I'm telling this story. I have never told this story in a church before. I have asked different people to come to Willow, Alaska, to finish the work. I have had people say they would come, yet not one has followed through on his commitment." He added again, "I still don't know why I am telling this now." At this point my dad started crying and went outside of the church. My mom wondered what was wrong, so she started praying for my dad.

As Brother Palmer left his rabbit trail and returned to his planned message, my mom heard in her heart a message she knew was from God: "I WANT YOU TO GO!"

When my dad came back into the church, he slid a note to my mom, which read, "Are you ready to go where God leads?"

She looked at my dad and nodded her head "Yes." She already knew they would be going to Alaska!

When Brother Palmer finished preaching, he called people

forward to pray. My dad and mom went to pray at the front of the church. As they were there, Mr. Palmer came up to my dad and said, "Brother, I don't know you, but God has a special call on your life." My dad told him that he and my mom were supposed to go to Alaska.

After the prayer service was over, my parents were visiting with others at the church. They were so surprised to hear that my mom's mother, my mom's sister and my mom's best friend Sue had all felt God put on their heart that my parents were to go to Alaska. This was a great confirmation because they had not told anyone about going to Alaska except Mr. Palmer. My mom said this particular incident was the clearest she has ever heard God put something on her heart in her entire life. My parents were in their early 20's, had been married less than two years and had never built anything before, yet both felt strongly that God had called them to go to Alaska.

My parents were ready to leave the next day, yet Brother Palmer gave them some great advice regarding preparing for the trip. It was winter, they had no money and a very old car that would probably not make it through Canada. Over the next several months, God completely provided without the indebtedness: a newer car and a trailer to haul their belongings as well as money for the trip. God even provided a minister friend who lived in Alaska but was visiting Texas to travel with them to help drive to Alaska.

When they arrived in Alaska, Melvin Stein, who had heard they were coming, allowed my parents to stay in his mobile home "rent-free." Melvin lived in Anchorage during the school year and lived in Talkeetna, which is north of Willow, while clearing his land in the summers. There was no running water in the mobile home, so my parents took five gallon cans to a filling station and then brought the water back to the trailer. The first thing my dad built was an outhouse (an outdoor toilet). My mom said it was quite a frigid experience going to the bathroom there when it was sixty degrees below zero!

One of the men who attended the church worked at a lumber yard, and he helped my parents choose a plan to build an A-frame building for the church. There was not enough cash for the materials, so a lady from Spenard Chapel loaned my parents $2,500 so the church could be built. The man at the lumber yard also made sure there were enough supplies for the project.

One morning my dad told my mom that they needed to go to Anchorage to get building supplies, but they only had five dollars left from donations. My mom said they had no flour, sugar, milk, meat, eggs, fruit or vegetables in the trailer. They had nothing to eat and only five dollars to their name. My dad suggested they wait until the mail came in case someone had mailed a donation. Nothing came in the mail, so they used the five dollars to put gas in the car to travel to Anchorage. When they picked up the building supplies, the man at the lumber yard took them out for lunch. He didn't know they had no money for food.

On the way home from Anchorage, they stopped at two different churches where they knew the pastors and some of the people. The churches had set up boxes with their names on them so people could donate food to my parents, yet when they checked this time there was no food in the boxes at either church. My mom said it was very quiet going back to the mobile home in Willow because they both knew there was no food there. They were not sure what to do other than pray.

When they unlocked the door of the mobile home, they found three large boxes full of groceries—Bisquick, canned fruit and vegetables, sugar, powdered milk as well as all kinds of goodies! They simply stood there, praised the Lord and cried! They knew that Melvin was the only other person who had a key to the place, yet they had not told him of their need for food. Later, they saw him to thank him for the food and to explain that they had no food in the house.

He said, "I was bringing the food home from the mountains, so the bears wouldn't break into the cabin and tear up the place. As I was about to pass your driveway, it was so strong on my heart from God to stop that I had to leave the food for you."

My mom said of the provisions they received, "I learned when God is all you have, God is enough!"

My parents were in Willow, Alaska, for two and a half years. During that time the church building was completed and all paid for. My mom says the miracle is how God provided the money to pay for it. The highest income for my parents in one of the years was $2,500. Only a small number of people attended the church, and even fewer gave money; God still provided for ALL of their needs. My brother, Barty, was born in Alaska in 1964, and God even provided the money from donations to pay the hospital bill!

As my parents were preparing to leave Alaska to move back

to Texas, they realized Canada required them to show proof of having the sum of $350 to enter the country so the border patrol would know that travelers would have the funds required to make it through to the United States. My parents added up all the money from every place they could find and still didn't have enough to satisfy the Canadian border patrol. My dad came up with the plan to arrive at the border at night, and he would meet with the patrol while my mom prayed. By faith, he believed they would be permitted to go through Canada. As planned, they headed to the border at night, my dad went inside, and my mom prayed that the patrol officers would not even ask how much money my parents had.

When my dad returned to the car, he said, "They did not even ask me about our money!!" Thus, they made it back to Texas, where I was born a couple of years later.

My mom said she could write her own book to tell of God's faithfulness to provide for her over the last fifty-plus years, yet she is glad to give God glory for this story. Willow Chapel has changed its name to New Life Christian Center and is bearing fruit over fifty years later from the initial work my parents planted. My mom found out several years ago that the church gave $100,000 to missionaries in one year in the 1990's, which was very inspiring to her. She wanted me to reiterate the saying which she learned and has lived by: "When God is all you have, God is enough!"

It is God-ordained that my parents had a life-changing experience while building an A-frame chapel in the early 60's. Almost fifty years later I had the profound life experience in the

A-frame chapel, which God used to motivate me to write this book. They planted the seeds and watered them; we are reaping a bountiful harvest!

This is a photograph of the A-frame chapel my parents built in Willow, Alaska.

58 | God's Eye Is on the Sparrow

*Although my experience with the sparrow
happened in the summer,
here's Windermere Chapel in the winter.*

CHAPTER FOUR

My Divine Provision Story

My Own Story

God has provided for me in many ways throughout my life. Some of the several examples of His divine provision include food, protection, finances for college, personal development and starting businesses.

My parents have told me that I was an unplanned child and conceived while they were using birth control. By the way, this fact was not told to me in an unkind way; rather, they shared the simple facts in a more cut-and-dried way. My mom had said she did not want to have another child until they could afford it. Neither of my parents were working full-time when I was born, yet God provided for everything. I carry no hard feelings toward my parents or their way of explaining my conception. I know that God planned me! My parents were experiencing difficult financial times before I was born, and my coming into the world only added extra pressure.

Later my dad was the full-time pastor of a very small non-denominational church in Las Vegas, Nevada, and my parents lived on a meager income when I was a baby. My father started working as a janitor at a large retail store at night to supplement

*Here's the Dearing family in the early 70's.
I'm the one with the coat of many colors.*

his income because the church had fewer than fifty parishioners. As a result, he was not readily available during the early years of my life. My mom mostly stayed home to care for us when we lived in Las Vegas, except for a few years when she worked outside the home for a Christian radio station.

As I noted, things were very tight financially for my parents when I was a child. Many of the clothes I wore were my brother's hand-me-downs, or they were made by my mom, or they were a donation from another family. The same was true for our toys. My brother and I were on the free lunch program at school due to our low family income level, and we lived in a trailer park. In particular, I vividly remember one time when I was not yet ten years old that we didn't have food for dinner. My parents simply had us bow our heads and pray. Thirty or so minutes later, someone brought some groceries to our door, saying that God had put our family on his heart. God always provided for us.

When I was a sophomore or junior in high school in Arnett, Oklahoma, my dad became disabled with myotonic muscular dystrophy and lost his pastoral position. Because our family lived in the parsonage next to the church, we also lost our housing. As a result, my family faced a particularly tough time financially because my dad did not qualify for social security disability until more than a year later. My mom was able to secure some work at the school cafeteria and also drove a school bus, but my dad never worked again. God provided food and money in numerous ways at key times at this period of life; we had exactly what we needed.

My brother, Barty Dearing, who is three years older than I am, drew the adjacent picture of this bird with colored pencils when we were in high school.

During my first years of high school, I was desperately trying to fit in and be accepted by the other students because our family had moved from out of state. Even as I watched my parents face this time of financial crisis, instead of contributing, I significantly increased my efforts to be more like my peers. Most of them tended to party and drink an excessive amount.

I remember one time at the end of my junior year when some other high schoolers and I had far too much to drink. Someone came up with the brilliant idea to float down the Canadian River on inner-tubes when it was in flood stage. To this day, I am not exactly sure how it happened, but I nearly drowned. In my drunken state, I somehow became trapped in an eddy created by some trapped tree branches in the river. Thankfully, I popped up from under the branches and water, and my life was spared. God miraculously freed me from the entrapment and kept me from drowning! This near-death experience shook me up so much that I vowed to stop drinking alcohol from that day forward. I also quit hanging around my high school peers who were getting drunk so much.

As a result of God's wakeup call, I straightened up that summer and became serious about my life. It became apparent that God had plans for my life. I had no serious thoughts of going to college until I almost drowned and started attending the Assembly of God church in Woodward, Oklahoma. Until that significant emotional experience, I was more or less floating through life without direction (pun intended) than having a plan. Because of my goofing off, I had never before tried to earn good grades, but then I set a goal of earning all A's during my senior year of high school to prove to myself and to my parents that I was college-bound. Once I set my mind to it, I was able to accomplish this goal.

One of those who made a tremendous difference in my life during high school was Jim Parham, my scoutmaster and band teacher. Mr. Parham helped me become an Eagle Scout and learn to play the drums. God used him mightily through his advice and mentorship in helping me not to choose more wrong roads at critical times in high school. God has always provided key mentors throughout my life, and beyond a shadow of a doubt, I would not be where I am without them.

Then I received some small scholarships and grants and scraped together enough of my savings to enroll at Evangel College (now Evangel University) in Springfield, Missouri. I worked part-time while attending school full-time. In spite of living quite frugally, I still came to the end of my first year of classes, owing the school a balance that needed to be paid off before I could enroll for the next year. I quickly realized I would not be able to earn what I needed by working over the summer on the farm owned by my great-aunt and great-uncle. I had worked for them while I was in high school, and I recognized that I would not make enough to pay off both the balance owed and have enough left to enroll in the fall semester. When I sought help at the financial aid office, I was told they had done what they could do. I remember crying out to God in prayer for help because I knew that I was supposed to be in college.

Several weeks later, the Varsity Internship Program, a division of Thomas Nelson Publishers, came to the Evangel campus. This program of selling books had never before been introduced at Evangel. The director, Sonny Crews, explained that students could work on a summer internship selling books door-to-door, and that these students would average $3,000 in profit for a summer's work. This amount was much more than I could hope to make back home on the farm, so I told my parents I wanted to do it. My dad did not think the internship was a good idea, yet somehow I convinced my parents it was an answer to my prayers, so they finally gave their consent.

I received one week of sales training in Nashville, Tennessee, and with less than a hundred dollars to my name, I travelled to West Virginia to sell books for twelve weeks. I knew I had to sell these books in order to earn enough money for food, gas, and a place to stay as well as make some money for college. If I was unsuccessful, I knew I would have to face my dad and tell him that I had failed.

Once I arrived in West Virginia, I remember crying at the prospect of having to go knock on doors, yet God helped me persevere. I determined to stay no matter what transpired. Anyway, I wouldn't have had the money for the gas to drive the 1,000-plus miles back home, without asking my parents for it, and that request simply was not going to happen. As I continued to persistently knock on doors, God kept providing a sale here and a sale there. The company had taught us to work a minimum of twelve and a half hours a day, six days per week and to set weekly goals as well as goals for each morning, afternoon, and evening.

The Varsity Internship Program managers were key in teaching me the importance of planting ideas in my mind that would bear much fruit in achievement. One of the books they instructed me to read that summer was *Life Is Tremendous* by Charles Jones. The more I worked, the better I became at asking questions that helped me to understand what people needed. That first year in 1986, I ended up being the number-six rookie and earning $7,500 in twelve weeks. What a miracle! At the end of the summer, I found out that I had received an Army ROTC scholarship, but the Varsity Internship Program wanted me to return as a student manager to recruit students to go with me the next year. I did not really feel that I had what it took to be a manager, yet I had made so much money that I knew I had to try. I turned down the ROTC scholarship and continued to work with the Varsity Internship Program.

The next school year, I recruited five students to sell books door-to-door with me; however, only three lasted the whole summer. I ended up making $12,000 that summer. The next school year, I recruited twelve students to sell books, and our team broke the company record for sales as a student-led team.

I earned $18,000 that summer. The fourth school year, I worked so hard recruiting ten students that I was diagnosed with mononucleosis and missed the first two weeks of selling for the summer. With God's help, I still earned $15,000 in ten weeks that summer. I was the first person in the history of the company to earn the Triple Crown award twice in a row, which required a certain level of recruiting, sales and savings. God not only provided a college internship where I ran my own business to help me pay my way through school, I also learned character lessons and proper attitudes that continue to guide my life to this day.

> "You will be the same person five years from now, with two exceptions: the people you meet and the books you read."   – Charles "Tremendous" Jones

I earned accounting and management degrees with a marketing minor from Evangel University. I am very grateful how the professors at Evangel helped me integrate my faith with my academic learning. My favorite class my first year was business and personal finances—dealing with investments, insurance, budgeting and financial planning. From that time forward, I started to see that I could be involved with finances in a different way. I had enrolled in college to become an accountant, yet something kept drawing me back to business and personal finances.

While in college, I visited Larry Burkett's headquarters at Christian Financial Concepts because he was one of the most respected Christian authors and speakers on finances at the time. I read and listened to everything I could find by him since I wanted to figure out how to work with people in the area of their money. The only problem I found was that the financial advisor position did not receive a salary, and I had a great fear of trying to build a business.

I hated the idea of selling books each summer without knowing how much I would make, so upon graduation, I accepted a salaried job replete with a company car with Eastman Kodak. I started in Springfield, Missouri, and was tasked with selling large equipment for them. I received all kinds of training from Kodak, which was great, yet I still did not like what I did for the company because I was trying to sell high-end equipment. Quite simply, I did not feel like I was helping people. I did take a transfer to St. Louis with Kodak in case it was the undeveloped territory in Springfield rather than my disgust for what I was doing as a career that was causing the problem. I soon realized that I was again thinking about personal finances and how I could get into the financial industry.

Then my dad unexpectedly died on July 4, 1992, at the age of fifty-two, a couple of years after I graduated from college. He had developed pneumonia in the hospital after having some tests run, and due to the myotonic muscular dystrophy, he did not have the strength to fight it off. Our family believes on the day that my dad died (Independence Day), God helped him receive freedom from the pain he had been experiencing the last years of his life.

When I sat down to help my mom sort through the finances, I found out that they had no savings, no retirement, no life insurance—nothing. My mom even asked people to give donations to the funeral home in lieu of flowers because there was no money to bury my dad. She ended up selling her house to keep from losing it because my dad had said that mortgage life insurance was too expensive.

Less than a year after losing my dad, I started a financial business in May 1993 with a mission to help people avoid the financial holocaust my family experienced. In 1994 I met with John Ashcroft, the former governor of Missouri, when he was preparing to run for senator of Missouri. His dad had been the president of Evangel where I had attended college, and he graciously met with me to network. He really encouraged me to share my story with others about why I felt God's calling to be in the financial industry. His encouragement greatly helped. However, the first five years were still brutal because I was not from the St. Louis area, and I found it was very difficult to get people to meet with me about their finances. Through the grace of God, knowing my purpose, hard work, and persistence, I survived the times where most people fail as financial advisors and began building a successful business.

God has used the challenging times I have faced in my life to have a different perspective in dealing with others regarding what they are encountering. Over time, the business mission changed from having people avoid what my family experienced to finding out the dreams of clients, then doing everything possible to help them reach their dreams. In the process of helping the clients reach their dreams, we set up plans to avoid the financial challenges my family faced.

I was on top of the world in the year 2000. In March of 2000, I had heard a recording by Jim Rohn called "The Challenge to Succeed in the 90's" and in May of 2000, I had read that book that I mentioned earlier by Brian Klemmer called *If How-To's Were Enough, We Would All Be Skinny, Rich & Happy* that literally rocked my world (Now I've read this book 26 times!). Things were going great financially as a result of improving my attitude and perspective starting with having daily devotionals and implementing what I had learned from Jim Rohn and Brian Klemmer. The business doubled in 2000, and my wife and I were able to buy our dream home.

In 2003 I hired a personal life coach, Dr. Tom Hill, who was instrumental in helping me enhance my life plans by moving from one-year goals to a six-year plan to reach God's perfect plan for my life. I began thinking bigger, looking for predictable miracles and achieving more in my life as a result of his coaching. At the end of 2003, I attended a personal growth workshop held through Klemmer and Associates called "Personal Mastery." I created so much value in my life at this workshop that I attended their following workshops, including "Advanced Leadership" in San Francisco, "Heart of the Samurai" in San Diego, and "Samurai Camp" in Phoenix. I began hosting Klemmer and Associates workshops in the St. Louis area, and I helped hundreds of people attend ten workshops over the next few years. Brian Klemmer became a close mentor who also invested into my life greatly. In the spring of 2006, Klemmer and Associates bestowed on me their first ever awarded PhD in Leadership and Personal Development based on the work I did with orphanages in Moldova and Ukraine. So many things were going well, and I attributed it all to God's blessings in my life!

In 2007 I created an agreement with God called the "Divine Partnership Agreement" (see sample on adjacent page). Law and accounting firms often have the senior partners obtain the clients while the junior partners do the bulk of the service and organizational work. I realized that I needed to make God the senior partner of the business, while I served as the junior partner. God was to be in charge of getting new clients, marketing the business, providing a vision for the business, and blessing the business. I was to be in charge of serving the clients, strategizing with them while listening to what God wanted me to do and being faithful to do those things.

Yes, this model is probably different from any other you have heard about in business, but it works for me because God gave me the idea. I do no prospecting myself. God continues to prompt people to call me. When I do meet with a prospective client, I do not try to convince the person to work with me. I simply lay out how I work. If it is a win/win relationship, I am willing to move forward. Otherwise, I acknowledge that the client will be better served working with someone else.

> "Trust in God, not in man, not in circumstances, not in any of your own exertions, but real trust in God, and you will be helped in your various necessities... Not in circumstances, not in natural prospects, not in former donors, but solely in God. This is just that which brings the blessing. If we say we trust in Him, but in reality do

DIVINE PARTNERSHIP AGREEMENT

This PARTNERSHIP AGREEMENT is made on _____, 20___ between _____ and God.

1. NAME AND BUSINESS. The parties hereby form a partnership under the name of _____ to conduct a business forever. The principal office of the business shall be in _____'s heart.

2. TERM. The partnership shall begin on _____, 20___, and shall continue forever.

3. CAPITAL. The capital of the partnership shall be contributed by the partners as follows: Acknowledgement and belief that the blood of Christ was shed for my sins. Thus, _____'s only capital commitment is to accept Christ's free gift.

4. PROFIT AND LOSS. The net profits of the partnership shall be managed by _____ on God's behalf. There will be various audits to check _____'s stewardship as well as a final day of accounting when _____ dies. _____ agrees to give _____ % of the profits of the partnership to further God's Kingdom.

5. MANAGEMENT DUTIES AND RESTRICTIONS. The partners shall list below the management duties of the partnership business, and each partner shall devote his entire efforts in the conduct of the business.

GOD'S PART	_____'s PART
(Senior Partner)	(Junior Partner)
_____	_____
_____	_____
_____	_____
_____	_____

6. DEATH. Upon the death of _____ in the natural, _____ will join said Divine Partner forever in eternity. Thus, continuing the enjoyment of the fruit of this Divine Partnership.

Executed this _____ day of _____, 20_____ in _____ [city/state].

_____ _____

(THIS IS NOT TO BE USED AS A LEGAL DOCUMENT.)

not, then God, taking us at our word, lets us see that we do not really confide in Him; and hence failure arises. On the other hand, if our trust in the Lord is real, help will surely come...We serve a God with unlimited resources and power, all the resources of the Godhead are at our disposal." – George Müller

Also in 2007, I attended a workshop by Bill and Linda McGrane in Ohio called "Move Into Your Greatness." This workshop helped me connect with God and myself in a greater capacity, which allowed me to love my wife more unconditionally. When my wife attended the same workshop several years later, our marriage was strengthened as a result of us both living based on the principles.

In the fall of 2008, I attended a workshop by Lance Wallnau called the "Believer's Edge." Lance is a consultant and a speaker who has been instrumental in sharing the story of the Seven Mountains, which are the seven domains that shape a culture and the minds of a nation. These mind molders are family, religion/faith, education, government/law, media/news, arts/entertainment and business/economics. I was introduced to Lance through Kirk Metz, a great friend of mine I had met in 2004 at the "Heart of the Samurai" workshop with Brian Klemmer. Kirk is one of the most amazing "Connectors" on the planet. Kirk had also introduced Brian Klemmer to Lance, which developed into quite a friendship between all of us. From my work with Klemmer & Associates, I was able to speak at the "Believer's Edge" workshop regarding taking responsibility for our actions.

I found it interesting that Lance's mentor is Bill McGrane, and Kirk introduced me to each of them on separate occasions. I have been so encouraged about what I have been able to learn and the people I have been able to meet at all of the workshops I have attended!

Another workshop I attended in the fall of 2008 was in the St. Louis area by Craig Hill from Family Foundations International called "Ancient Paths 1" to keep investing in my personal development. The workshop walked me through the seven times in life when someone received blessing or hurt ("curses") from their parents and those they loved. The facilitators were very instrumental in helping me forgive myself and others for hurts that had happened in my past.

As a result of what I had learned in the Ancient Paths 1 (AP1) workshop, I determined to go to the classes called "Process Groups." This group met weekly six times to go into more depth with the material from the Ancient Paths 1 workshop and allow for extra ministry time. My heart was so touched with the AP1 workshop and the Process Group meetings that I then attended every workshop (eight more) that was offered through Family Foundations and experienced additional breakthroughs in each one. From there I joined the ministry team where I have continued to serve to this day. These workshops were a key factor in God's helping me to hear from Him better, strengthen my marriage and improve my life. I am reminded of the saying that I heard from Jim Rohn in 2000: "If you will change, everything will change for you." At many times I looked at others and wanted them to change so things would get better for our friendship or relationship. Thankfully, God helped me to see that I needed to change, and that understanding has made all of the difference.

> "It is not the mountain we conquer, but ourselves."
> – Sir Edmund Hillary
> (1919–2008)
> New Zealander, humanitarian
> First man to summit Mt. Everest

In December 2011 it started becoming clear to me that I was being led by God to start a new financial firm called "Wealth Ambassadors." Following through was a challenging decision because, at the same time, I had been a founding member of a rapidly growing financial firm since September 1994. That firm had grown from 16 of us located in St. Louis to 150 people strategically placed between St. Louis, Kansas City, and Omaha by the time I left the firm in July 2012.

A profound event happened in January 2012 as one of many confirmations of my need to resign. At a breakfast I was talking with a close mentor (not affiliated with the company) about feeling the urge to leave the firm. I shared at lunch with my wife that same day about my breakfast meeting. We were both very moved in our hearts that we were to step out in faith to start a new financial company and write this book about the sparrow experience. The picture of a bird in a cage came to my mind and to open the door to let the bird fly free. The bird could sing, yet it had limited movement in the cage. As I told my wife about the caged bird, God put on my heart that I was the bird in the cage and that He had opened the door of my bird cage. God was saying in my heart FLY, FLY, FLY! You are FREE as a bird!

I remembered that afternoon that the bird in the chapel was somewhat in a cage and that God had said that I was that bird. My devotions that very night were from Psalm 124. In verse seven and eight it says, *"we are like a bird escaped from the snare of the fowlers; the snare is broken, and we have escaped! Our help is in the name of the Lord, who made heaven and earth."* These kinds of occurrences where something took place during the day then my devotions dealt with the same event that night have happened hundreds of times in the last fifteen years.

Thankfully, this is one of the dozens of times I wrote down in my journal exactly what happened, which surely emphasizes the importance of journaling and capturing what God is doing in our lives so we and others can be encouraged in the future. I immediately started making preparations to "fly free" to the new company that God was having me start.

I am truly grateful for how God has provided abundantly beyond all I could ask or imagine since following His guidance throughout my life and especially regarding starting the company, Wealth Ambassadors. The beautiful thing is that, based on Acts 10:34 and 35, God is not a respecter of persons. What He has done for George Müller, Sister Barney, Sonny Brown, countless others, and me, He can and will do for you—if you will simply ask. I believe these verses in Luke 11:9 and 10 (AMP) say it best:

"So I say to you, Ask and keep on asking and it shall be given you; seek and keep on seeking and you shall find; knock and keep on knocking and the door shall be opened to you. [10]For everyone who asks and keeps on asking receives; and he who seeks and keeps on seeking finds; and to him who knocks and keeps on knocking, the door shall be opened."

"Call upon Me in the day of trouble; I shall rescue you, and you will honor Me."

– Psalm 50:15 (NASB)

CONCLUSION

Fly Free!

My prayer has been that all of these words will help you understand what God's Word says—His provision is not determined by our efforts and striving when we are His children. Rather, He provides for us unconditionally—as He does for the sparrows. I want to share a poem I found that captures my thoughts about divine provision.

God's Provision

A Christian poem about God's providing for our needs based on Matthew 6:31-34:

We so often do not trust in God
    And lack faith that He will provide,
    We worry, we fret, and we fuss so much,
    In His blessings, we do not abide

For how can the hand of Almighty God
    Stretch forth with all that we need
    If we are not even expecting it
    And have doubt instead of belief?

78 | God's Eye Is on the Sparrow

His Word has said so many times
    That He will provide for His children
    He won't leave us to go begging for bread,
    But feed us from the storehouse of heaven.

Look at the sparrows, the birds of the air,
    Are we not worth more than they?
    And consider the lilies; see how they grow,
    How magnificently they are arrayed

So much more than the lilies of the field,
    Our clothing, will He not provide?
    More than the sparrows that feed from His hand,
    Our food, He will not deny

We really must believe in God's provision
    As sure as the fresh morning dew,
    For He already knows just what are our needs
    And He will always come through.

© By M.S. Lowndes
Used by permission.

    May this book make a difference for you, a new beginning in following God's way. If you will go back through the lessons from the sparrow and ask yourself, "What can I apply to my life?" Write down what God shows you. Then this book will go from being a nice read to making a lasting impact.

Conclusion | 79

If you begin seeking Scriptures for God to guide you, you will find them. Proverbs 3:32 says, *"His confidential communion and secret counsel are with the* [uncompromisingly] *righteous (those who are upright and in right standing with Him)."* In John 14 Jesus said that He was giving us the Holy Spirit who would be with us at all times. The Holy Spirit would be our Comforter, Counselor, Helper, Intercessor, Advocate, Strengthener and Standby, who would teach us all things. The Holy Spirit would also cause us to recall all that Jesus told us. Jesus said in verses 12-17 if we believe steadfastly that we can do the things Jesus did and greater things because He was going to the Father.

I pray that you will go after God with all of your heart, soul, mind and strength. It is my prayer that you will literally put God at the center of your life. May you learn that He wants to put things on your heart like never before in your life. May you fly out through the doors that God opens to your future!

Here's your open door!

Endnotes

Introduction
Mark 9:23 (ERV), *Jesus said to the father, "Why did you say 'if you can'? All things are possible for the one who believes."*

Chapter 1: Release of the Sparrow
Camp Windermere is located in Central Missouri on the Lake of the Ozarks. It can be found on the Internet at: http://windermereusa.org/

Worldwide Inventory Network is a 501(c)3, non-profit organization that receives excess inventory from companies and distributes it to other non-profits. It can be found on the Internet at: www.winwarehouse.org/

John 10:9 (NASB), *"I am the door; if anyone enters through Me, he will be saved, and will go in and out and find pasture."*

Revelation 3:20 (NASB), *"Behold, I stand at the door and knock; if anyone hears My voice and opens the door, I will come in to him and will dine with him, and he with Me."*

John 14:6 (NASB), *Jesus said to him, "I am the way, and the truth, and the life; no one comes to the Father but through Me."*

Chapter 2: Lessons From a Sparrow

Matthew 6:33 (KJV), *"But seek ye first the kingdom of God, and his righteousness, and all these things shall be added unto you."*

Books on Emotional Intelligence by Dr. Daniel Goleman include *Emotional Intelligence: Why It Can Matter More Than IQ; Working With Emotional Intelligence; Primal Leadership: Unleashing the Power of Emotional Intelligence;* and *Building Emotional Intelligence: Practices to Cultivate Inner Resilience in Children* (with Linda Lantieri)

Books/CDs by Brian Klemmer that deal with the subconscious mind include *If How To's Were Enough, We Would All Be Skinny, Rich and Happy; The Compassionate Samurai;* and *The*

Pursuit and Practice of Personal Mastery. Seminars and workshops by Brian Klemmer include Advanced Leadership, Heart of the Samurai and Samurai Camp.

Hebrews 13:5 (NASB), *Make sure that your character is free from the love of money, being content with what you have; for He Himself has said, "I WILL NEVER DESERT YOU, NOR WILL I EVER FORSAKE YOU."*

James 1:17 (NASB), *"Every good thing given and every perfect gift is from above, coming down from the Father of lights, with whom there is no variation or shifting shadow."*

John 10:10 (NASB), *"The thief comes only to steal and kill and destroy; I came that they may have life, and have it abundantly."*

What are some lessons that you learned from the story of the sparrow? If you would be so kind as to send them to us, we will include them in a section of our website so that others can also learn from them as well. You may visit the website at this address:

www.godseyeisonthesparrow.com
Click on "Lessons Learned."

You will have access to read the lessons of others as well.

Chapter 4: My Divine Provision Story

Myotonic Muscular Dystrophy is a disease that causes the muscles to break down such that the body is no longer able to function. More information can be found here: http://mda.org/disease/myotonic-muscular-dystrophy/types. My dad's disease happened to be adult-onset, yet there are multiple types.

I have mostly kept my vow to not drink alcohol over the last 30-plus years. A handful of times I have chosen to have a drink at a function many years ago, yet I have found that it is not my thing. I do not ever want to be in a situation where the alcohol has negatively influenced a decision I had to make, and I experience regret. I do not look down on anyone who chooses to drink alcohol. Each person has his own choices to make in life.

The Varsity Internship Program is still an option for college students to make money in the summers though it is no longer affiliated with Thomas Nelson Publishers:
http://varsityinternshipprogram.com/

Here's a free book on the life of George Müller if you would like to read more about him:
http://freepdfhosting.com/ab1749ecca.pdf.

The orphan organization he started (www.muller.org) is still active and has now served over 100,000 orphans. Many of his other online books, which are free as well, can be found here at this website:
http://www.georgemuller.org/home.html.

I would love to hear from you about how God has provided for you and/or how you are asking God to provide for you in the future. Please go to the following website: www.godseyeisonthesparrow.com and tell us about it. To share, click on "Provision Stories."

Conclusion: Fly Free!

For additional reading on the poem, "God's Provision," by M.S. Lowndes, please visit the website:
www.heavensinspirations.com/gods-provision.html
Used by permission. All rights reserved.

Windermere in the fall

Windermere in the spring with pink blooming tree

Made in the USA
Monee, IL
25 July 2024